ST. PAUL'S CATHEDRAL

Kaite Goldsworthy

MEDIA ENHANCED BOOKS
AV2 BY WEIGL™
ADDED VALUE • AUDIO VISUAL

www.av2books.com

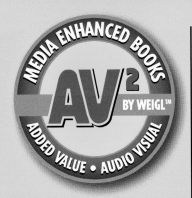

AV² provides enriched content that supplements and complements this book. Weigl's AV² books strive to create inspired learning and engage young minds in a total learning experience.

Your AV² Media Enhanced books come alive with...

Audio
Listen to sections of the book read aloud.

Key Words
Study vocabulary, and complete a matching word activity.

Go to **www.av2books.com**, and enter this book's unique code.

Video
Watch informative video clips.

Quizzes
Test your knowledge.

BOOK CODE

M 7 9 1 1 2 7

Embedded Weblinks
Gain additional information for research.

Slide Show
View images and captions, and prepare a presentation.

AV² by Weigl brings you media enhanced books that support active learning.

Try This!
Complete activities and hands-on experiments.

... and much, much more!

Published by AV² by Weigl
350 5th Avenue, 59th Floor
New York, NY 10118
Websites: www.av2books.com www.weigl.com

Library of Congress Cataloging-in-Publication Data
Goldsworthy, Kaite.
 St. Paul's Cathedral / Kaite Goldsworthy.
    pages cm -- (Houses of faith)
 Includes index.
 ISBN 978-1-4896-1154-3 (hardcover : alk. paper) -- ISBN 978-1-4896-1155-0 (softcover : alk. paper) --
ISBN 978-1-4896-1156-7 (single user ebk.) -- ISBN 978-1-4896-1157-4 (multi user ebk.)
 1. St. Paul's Cathedral (London, England)--Juvenile literature. 2. Architecture, Baroque--England--London--Juvenile literature. 3. Anglican church buildings--England--London--Juvenile literature. 4. London (England)--Buildings, structures, etc.--Juvenile literature. I. Title.
 NA5470.S5G65 2014
 726.609421'2--dc23

                          2014002149

Editor: Heather Kissock
Design: Mandy Christiansen

Printed in the United States of America in North Mankato, Minnesota
1 2 3 4 5 6 7 8 9 0 18 17 16 15 14

032014
WEP150314

Every reasonable effort has been made to trace ownership and to obtain permission to reprint copyright material. The publishers would be pleased to have any errors or omissions brought to their attention so that they may be corrected in subsequent printings.

Weigl acknowledges Getty Images, Alamy, and Dreamstime as its primary image suppliers for this title.

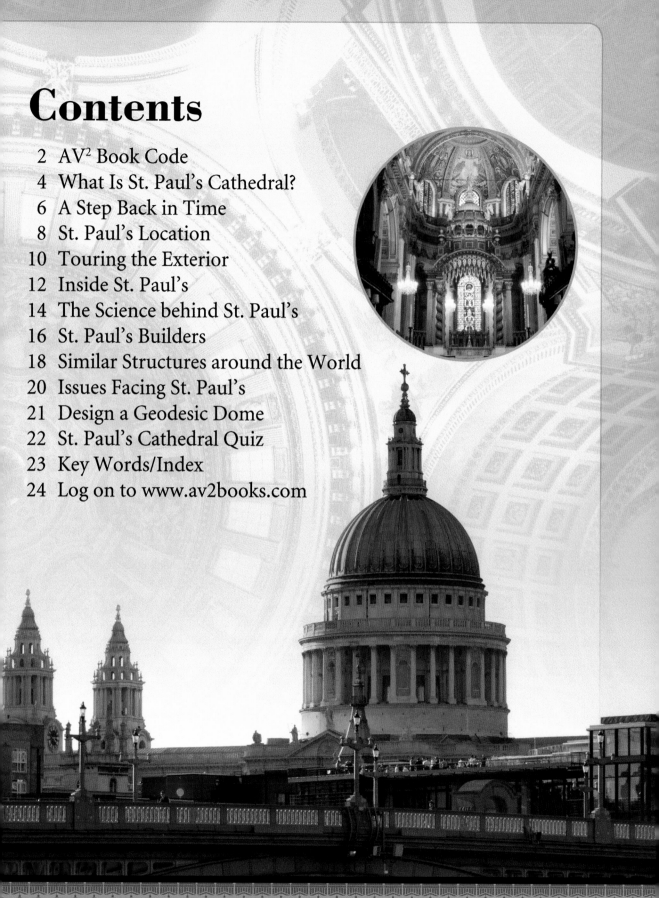

Contents

What Is St. Paul's Cathedral?

St. Paul's Cathedral appears to tower over the city of London, England. Its massive dome and tall **spires** form an integral part of the city's skyline. St. Paul's has been a focal point of the city since its completion in 1711. It is one of the largest Anglican cathedrals in England and serves as the **seat** for the bishop of London.

The cathedral was built after the Great Fire of London destroyed most of the city's buildings in 1666. St. Paul's was constructed to replace the church that had stood on the site before the fire. The job of designing the new cathedral fell to English **architect** Christopher Wren. The result is a structure built in the **English Baroque** style.

Even though St. Paul's Cathedral is in the heart of the city, it is surrounded by green space. The cathedral has its own gardens, and two parks lie to the south and southeast.

The Anglican Faith

Anglicanism is a form of Christianity. Christian religions are based on the teachings of a man, Jesus Christ, who is believed to have lived more than 2,000 years ago. In 1531, England's King Henry VIII formed the Church of England, which was the first Anglican church. Today, Anglicanism is the largest Christian religion in England. Followers of the Church of England share many beliefs with other Christians. They believe that Jesus was the son of God. The Bible, a holy book used for spiritual guidance, is at the center of the faith. Anglicans refer to the Bible for direction and guidance but are allowed flexibility in the way they practice their faith.

About **1 MILLION** people in the country of England attend a Church of England service each Sunday.

Anglican churches can be found in more than **160 COUNTRIES** around the world.

26 **BISHOPS AND ARCHBISHOPS** sit in the House of Lords. They work with the government of the United Kingdom to make laws.

There are **70** million+ Anglicans in the world.

A Step Back in Time

Plans had been in motion to renovate the old St. Paul's Cathedral before the Great Fire of London took place. The old St. Paul's stood on the site for almost 600 years, but had been damaged over the years by war and fires. It was in great need of repairs. Christopher Wren had already been hired to oversee the renovations. His plans included adding a large dome to the structure. The fire destroyed the cathedral before the renovations even started.

As part of rebuilding the city, King Charles II asked Wren to design a new cathedral to be built on the same site. Wren's first two designs were unsuccessful. One was considered too foreign in appearance. The other had funding problems.

CONSTRUCTION TIMELINE

1668 Christopher Wren is chosen to design a new St. Paul's Cathedral.

1672 Wren begins work on his next design, known as the Great Model. He spends 10 months designing it, and then a year building a model. Workers begin to measure and mark the ground for construction.

1675 Wren's third plan, known as the Warrant Design, is approved. The first foundation stone is laid on June 21.

| 1665 | 1668 | 1670 | 1673 | 1675 |

1666 The Great Fire of London destroys 80 percent of the city, including an older version of St. Paul's Cathedral.

1669 Wren completes his first design, but it is rejected.

1673 The plan for the Great Model is abandoned.

After almost nine years of work, Wren received approval on his third design, which was considered to be more English in appearance. The cathedral would not be completed until 35 years after the design approval. As it was being built, Christopher Wren made changes based on his second design, which he felt was better.

St. Paul's central location in London has made it a hub of activity for centuries.

1710 The construction of St. Paul's Cathedral is finally complete.

1698 Construction of the dome begins. The cathedral is now 98 feet (30 meters) tall.

| 1695 | 1700 | 1705 | 1710 | 1715 |

1697 Although construction is not yet complete, the first religious service is held in the cathedral.

1708 The dome is completed, and St. Paul's reaches its full height. The last brick is laid by the sons of Christopher Wren and the master **stonemason** on October 26.

1711 The British Parliament declares St. Paul's Cathedral officially finished.

St. Paul's Location

St. Paul's Cathedral is located on the north bank of the Thames River, which runs through the center of London. It sits on Ludgate Hill, the highest point in the City of London. The cathedral remains a visible part of the London skyline, even though it is now surrounded by modern skyscrapers and office buildings.

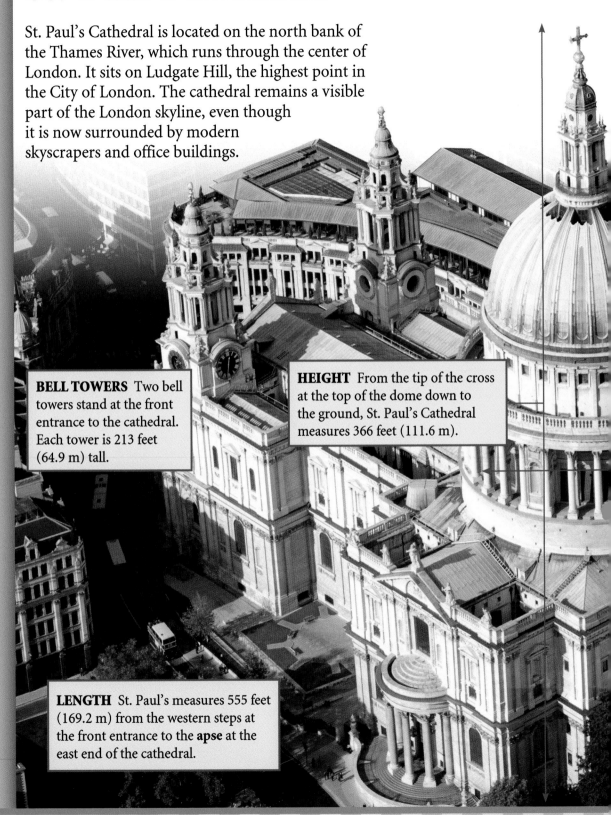

BELL TOWERS Two bell towers stand at the front entrance to the cathedral. Each tower is 213 feet (64.9 m) tall.

HEIGHT From the tip of the cross at the top of the dome down to the ground, St. Paul's Cathedral measures 366 feet (111.6 m).

LENGTH St. Paul's measures 555 feet (169.2 m) from the western steps at the front entrance to the **apse** at the east end of the cathedral.

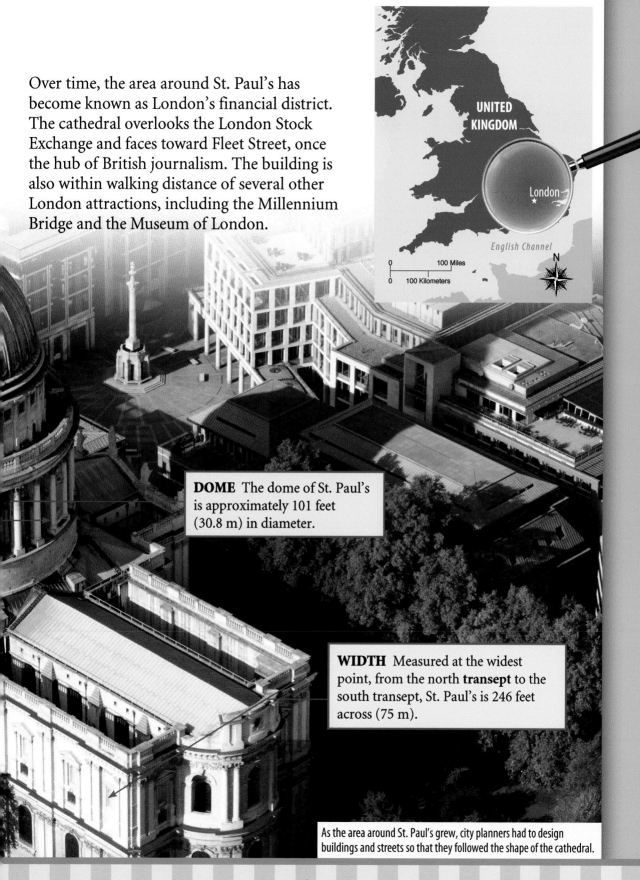

Over time, the area around St. Paul's has become known as London's financial district. The cathedral overlooks the London Stock Exchange and faces toward Fleet Street, once the hub of British journalism. The building is also within walking distance of several other London attractions, including the Millennium Bridge and the Museum of London.

UNITED KINGDOM

London

English Channel

0   100 Miles

0   100 Kilometers

N

DOME The dome of St. Paul's is approximately 101 feet (30.8 m) in diameter.

WIDTH Measured at the widest point, from the north **transept** to the south transept, St. Paul's is 246 feet across (75 m).

As the area around St. Paul's grew, city planners had to design buildings and streets so that they followed the shape of the cathedral.

Touring the Exterior

St. Paul's Cathedral is best known for its dome, but it also has many other features. Each helps to make the structure one of the most recognized cathedrals in the world.

WEST FRONT Most people enter St. Paul's through the west front. This is considered the cathedral's main entrance. The front of the cathedral has two levels, each featuring its own **colonnade**. Sitting on top of the second level colonnade is a **pediment** showing the **conversion** of St. Paul to Christianity. A sculpture of St. Paul stands above it.

TOWERS The main entrance is flanked by two tall towers. These towers house the bells of St. Paul's Cathedral. The southwest tower has a three-faced clock. Above the clock are four bells—Great Tom, Great Paul, and two quarter bells. Great Tom is rung every hour and to mark important events. Great Paul is the largest bell in Great Britain. It has a broken chime and can no longer be rung. There are twelve bells in the northwest tower. These are used for traditional **change ringing**.

DOME St. Paul's iconic dome is considered an architectural masterpiece. Its lead-encased exterior is topped with a ball and cross, which rests on a lantern. A colonnade circles the bottom of the dome. The dome features two outdoor viewing galleries. The Stone Gallery is found above the colonnade, at a height of 174 feet (53 m). The Golden Gallery is found at the top of the dome. At a height of 279 feet (85 m), it provides visitors with a breathtaking view of London.

The ball and cross topper weighs 8 tons (7.3 metric tons) and stands 23 feet (7 m) tall.

A statue of Queen Anne stands in front of St. Paul's. She was the queen of England when the cathedral was finished.

A pineapple sculpture sits at the top of each of the two bell towers. The pineapples symbolize peace, prosperity, and hospitality.

It would cost at least
$80 MILLION
to build St. Paul's
Cathedral today.

St. Paul's was London's **TALLEST**
BUILDING for more than **250**
years.

More than **1,000**
workers were hired to
build the cathedral.

Great Paul
weighs
37,483 pounds
(17,002 kg).

The face of each clock
on the southwest
tower is more than
16.4 feet
(5 m) in diameter.

People must climb
528 **steps to reach the**
Golden Gallery.

THE BELLS AT
ST. PAUL'S
RING IN THE
KEY OF B FLAT.

The cathedral's first bell,
known as The Banger,
was made in **1700**
and is still rung today.

The dome is believed
to weigh about
65,000 tons
(58,967 metric tons).

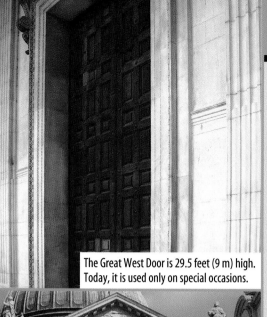

The Great West Door is 29.5 feet (9 m) high.
Today, it is used only on special occasions.

The pediment over the west entrance is known for its detail.
Showing St. Paul on his way to Damascus, the sculpture even
includes the rooftops of the city in the bottom left corner.

The 12 bells in the northwest tower are
rung three different times every Sunday.

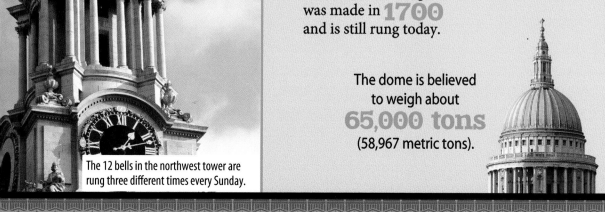

Inside St. Paul's

The interior of St. Paul's Cathedral was designed to inspire faith in all who entered. It is shaped like a cross to show its Christian heritage.

NAVE The **nave** of St. Paul's extends from the entrance to the dome, forming the longest part of the cross. It was designed to hold thousands of people and is now where the congregation sits. The long aisle is often used for processions to the high **altar**, which is located at the far end of the cathedral. The nave also provides access to several smaller chapels inside the cathedral. The Chapel of All Souls and St. Dunstan's Chapel are to the north of the nave. The Chapel of the Order of St. Michael and St. George is to the south.

TRANSEPTS The north and south transepts form the short arms of the cross. The north transept houses St. Paul's font, where people are baptised into the Anglican faith. The south transept features several memorials to well-known British military leaders. Both transepts have entrances to the **crypt**, where many notable Britons have been laid to rest.

QUIRE The quire forms the top of the cross. St. Paul's quire was the first part of the cathedral to be built. Today, it is where the clergy and the choir sit during religious services. The quire is also home to the cathedral's organ, which has five keyboards and more than 7,000 pipes. The high altar is made from marble and oak, and is found at the far end of the quire. The area in front of the altar is where mass and other ceremonies are led.

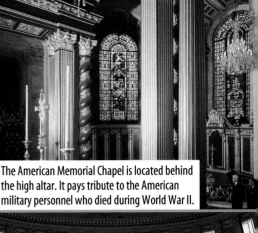

The American Memorial Chapel is located behind the high altar. It pays tribute to the American military personnel who died during World War II.

The Whispering Gallery circles the inside of the dome. The design of this gallery allows a whisper to be heard from the other side of the dome more than 100 feet (30 m) away.

The high altar was built in 1958. It is the cathedral's third high altar. It replaced an altar that was damaged during a bombing in World War II.

In the past, the nave was where the common people sat. It was blocked from the high altar by a large screen. Only the priests and the choir were permitted to see ceremonies being performed.

St. Paul's organ is the third largest in the country.

The dome is painted with eight scenes from the life of St. Paul. The scenes were painted by Sir James Thornhill in 1715 and took two years to complete.

There are more than
300 monuments
throughout the cathedral.

Visitors must climb  **259 steps to reach the Whispering Gallery.**

There are **859** seats in the nave of St. Paul's.

The cathedral's library contains more than **20,000** books.

 With its black and white tiles, the cathedral's floor looks like a large checkerboard.

1981
was the year Prince Charles married Lady Diana Spencer in the quire at St. Paul's.

Approximately
1 MILLION
tourists visit St. Paul's Cathedral each year.

The Science behind St. Paul's

Designing buildings requires an understanding of mathematics, science, and **engineering**. Besides being an architect, Christopher Wren was also a mathematician. He based much of his design for St. Paul's Cathedral on his knowledge in this area. From the construction of the dome to many of the designs inside the cathedral, math played an important role.

BUILDING ON A CURVE When designing the dome, Wren wanted to create a structure that could be seen from a great distance. He chose to make the dome **spherical** in shape. Spheres, however, are weak structures. On its own, the dome would not have been able to hold the lantern and the cross planned for the top of the cathedral. To provide support for the outer dome, Wren decided to add two other domes to the structure. Immediately underneath the outer dome is a cone-shaped dome made of brick. The arch of the cone rests just under the lantern. The third, inner dome is shaped as a catenary curve, which means its arch resembles that of a hanging chain. The shape of the arch allows the dome to support its own weight.

SUPPORTING THE LOAD The weight of the dome is pulled to the ground by gravity. To control the pressure of the weight, a series of supports were built. Underneath the outer dome are a circle of columns and several buttresses. A buttress is a brick or stone structure built against a wall to provide extra support. The force from the weight of the dome passes through the buttresses to eight large **piers** found on the ground floor of the cathedral. Wren used mathematics to calculate the best place for these supports to be built, as well as how tall and wide they should be to properly manage the weight of the dome.

SYMMETRY St. Paul's Cathedral was designed so that the two sides are symmetrical, or mirror each other. Wren used mathematics to determine the symmetry of his design. As a result, certain features are repeated on each side of the building. The north and south transepts, for instance, are positioned opposite each other and share similar features. Each side of the cathedral has the same number of pillars positioned in the same place. Aisles running along the sides of the building are also in perfect balance. The placement of these symmetrical features allows the center of the building to become the focal point.

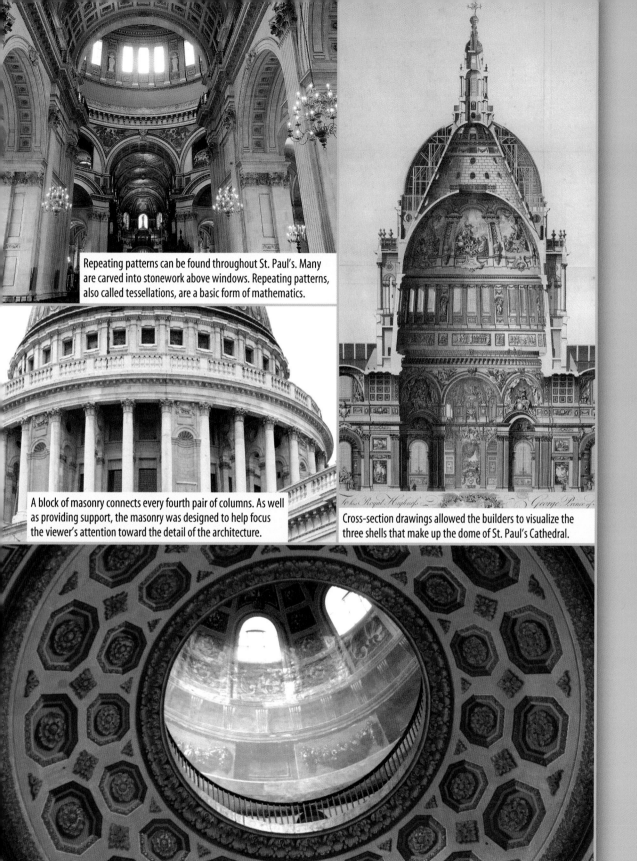

Repeating patterns can be found throughout St. Paul's. Many are carved into stonework above windows. Repeating patterns, also called tessellations, are a basic form of mathematics.

A block of masonry connects every fourth pair of columns. As well as providing support, the masonry was designed to help focus the viewer's attention toward the detail of the architecture.

Cross-section drawings allowed the builders to visualize the three shells that make up the dome of St. Paul's Cathedral.

The the inner dome is painted to look like it is open to the lantern on top. The opening actually shows the inside of the middle dome.

St. Paul's Builders

Although Christopher Wren was St. Paul's main architect, many other people contributed to the cathedral's construction. Some assisted Wren in bringing his vision to life. Others made their own unique contributions to the cathedral.

Christopher Wren Christopher Wren was born in England on October 20, 1632. After finishing primary school, he attended Oxford University, where he studied science and mathematics. He later became a professor of astronomy at Oxford. Wren's interest in architecture grew from his love of math, science, and engineering. He was named assistant to the **surveyor** of works by King Charles II in 1661. In 1669, Wren himself became the surveyor of works. Wren designed 52 churches in London, as well as many other buildings, including the Royal Chelsea Hospital and the Greenwich Royal Observatory. St. Paul's Cathedral is his best-known building. Wren died on February 25, 1723, twelve years after the completion of St. Paul's.

William Dickinson William Dickinson was born in 1671. His interest in architecture likely came from his father, who was responsible for tracking construction projects for the king. Dickinson began working for Christopher Wren in 1696. During the construction of St. Paul's, he was employed as a measuring clerk and surveyor. Dickinson drew many of the cathedral's floor plans and helped to organize the paving of the floor, as well as the steps to the western entrance. He later went on to work on many other buildings, often with Christopher Wren.

Christopher Wren was one of the first people to be buried in the crypt at St. Paul's. The tablet on his tomb states "Reader, if you seek a monument, look around you" in Latin.

Nicholas Hawksmoor Nicholas Hawksmoor was born in 1661. His interest in architecture was apparent early. When he was 18 years old, he moved to London to begin working as a clerk for Christopher Wren. Hawksmoor assisted Wren on several projects and was one of the **draftsmen** that helped draw detailed plans for St. Paul's Cathedral. Hawksmoor went on to design many structures as an architect in his own right. Outside of his work on St. Paul's, he is best known for designing the west towers of London's Westminster Abbey.

Grinling Gibbons Grinling Gibbons was born in the Netherlands and moved to England in the 1670s. By this time, he was already gaining a reputation as a skilled woodcarver. When Christopher Wren was given the job of rebuilding St. Paul's, he hired Gibbons to help with both the wood and stone work. Gibbons was responsible for carving the cathedral's wooden choir stalls, its organ case, and the bishop thrones. Many of the stone panels beneath the lower windows also showcase his work.

Francis Bird When people enter St. Paul's through the west entrance, they walk underneath a pediment showing the conversion of St. Paul. This sculpture is the work of Francis Bird. Bird is known as one of England's top sculptors of the 18th century. Bird was born in London in 1667. He received his training in continental Europe, **apprenticing** under master sculptors in Flanders and Rome. Upon his return to London, he began working as a sculptor at St. Paul's. Besides the pediment, Bird also sculpted the statue of Queen Anne that stands in front of the cathedral.

Similar Structures around the World

The Baroque period of architecture lasted from the 16th to 18th century. Its popularity in England, however, lasted for only a few decades, from about 1690 to 1730. During this time, several important cathedrals and churches were built. While these buildings share the lavish curves, lines, and colors of their European counterparts, they tend to show more restraint in their design.

St. George in the East Church

BUILT: 1714–1729
LOCATION: London, England
DESIGN: Nicholas Hawksmoor
DESCRIPTION: St. George in the East Church is best known for its four "pepperpot" **turrets**, which are located behind the central tower at the front of the building. Each turret contains a spiral staircase that, at one time, led to galleries overlooking the congregation. When originally built, the church had nine entrances for people from different social classes to enter. Today, most of these entrances have been turned into windows.

St. George in the East was one of 50 churches planned for the Greater London area in the 1700s. It was part of an initiative to promote Anglicanism in the country.

St. John's Church

BUILT: 1728
LOCATION: London, England
DESIGN: Thomas Archer
DESCRIPTION: St. John's Church is considered a prime example of English Baroque architecture. It is known for its symmetry and ornate **classical** features that include both pediments and columns. The church is sometimes referred to as Queen Anne's footstool. Legend has it that, when Queen Anne was asked what she wanted the church to look like, she kicked over a footstool and said, "Like that." The church's four towers are said to resemble the upturned legs of a footstool.

Following a bomb attack during World War II, St. John's Church was restored for use as a concert hall. Today, it hosts a variety of musical performances.

St. Mary Woolnoth is different from most churches in that its heavy appearance emphasizes the downward force of gravity instead of the upward pull of heaven.

St. Mary Woolnoth Church

BUILT: 1716
LOCATION: London, England
DESIGN: Nicholas Hawksmoor
DESCRIPTION: St. Mary Woolnoth Church is one of Nicholas Hawksmoor's most compact churches. The church is known for its almost fortress-like appearance. The ground level is built as a square block, a pattern repeated in the upward-reaching turrets. Still, the church possesses features consistent with the English Baroque style, including the pediment and columns found on the **facade**. Its interior contradicts the harsh exterior with its open and airy space.

Issues Facing St. Paul's

St. Paul's Cathedral is more than 300 years old. Although it was built to last, many of the issues facing the cathedral are related to age. Older buildings often need extra care and attention to maintain them for the future.

WHAT IS THE ISSUE?

The climate and pollution of London can damage the materials used to build the cathedral.

Over time, cracks have appeared in the stonework.

EFFECTS

St. Paul's Cathedral had become dark and blackened over time.

Cracks can lead to water damage. This could create larger structural issues for the building.

ACTION TAKEN

A 15-year cleaning and repair program of St. Paul's Cathedral was completed in 2011. It was the first time the cathedral had been fully cleaned inside and outside. More than 150,000 stones were cleaned as part of the program.

As part of the 2011 repairs, the west front entrance to the cathedral was restored, and **cornices** were repaired to prevent future water damage.

Design a Geodesic Dome

St. Paul's Cathedral is known for its tall dome. Various types and shapes of domes are used in construction. One common type of dome used today is the geodesic dome. This type of dome can be made up of triangles or polygons. The geodesic dome was invented more than 50 years ago and is often used for structures that need to be large and lightweight, such as sports arenas. Follow the instructions below to create a tasty version of a geodesic dome.

Materials

- 11 gumdrops

- 25 toothpicks that are pointed at both ends

Instructions

1. Use gumdrops to connect five toothpicks in a pentagon shape. This will be the base of the dome.

2. Use two toothpicks and one gumdrop to make a triangle on one side of the base.

3. Repeat, making triangles all around the pentagon-based shape.

4. Use toothpicks to connect the gumdrops at the tops of the triangles. Push one toothpick into each of the top gumdrops.

5. Use the last gumdrop to connect these toothpicks at the top.

6. Try testing the dome's strength by pressing down on one point of its many triangles. What does it do?

7. Using extra gumdrops and toothpicks, make a box. Press down on one of the points of the box. What does it do? How does this compare to the triangle?

St. Paul's Cathedral Quiz

Q What type of curve was used to create the inner dome of St. Paul's Cathedral?

A A catenary curve

Q How much does the dome of St. Paul's Cathedral weigh?

A 65,000 tons (58,967 metric tons)

Q Who designed St. Paul's Cathedral?

A Christopher Wren

Q Which part of St. Paul's Cathedral has 259 steps leading up to it?

A The Whispering Gallery

Key Words

altar: an elevated structure where religious ceremonies are performed

apprenticing: training under someone who is skilled in a trade

apse: the semi-circular area in a church, often at the east end, where the altar is usually placed

architect: a person who designs buildings

change ringing: ringing different bells in a constant order

classical: relating to Greek or Latin culture

colonnade: a series of columns placed at regular intervals

conversion: changing a faith or belief

cornices: ornamental moldings at the top of a wall or building

crypt: an underground room below a church used for burial

draftsmen: people who make detailed or technical drawings

engineering: the application of scientific principles to the design of structures

English Baroque: a style of architecture popular in the 1600s and 1700s, known for its ornate detail

facade: the principal front of a building

nave: the central part of a church where the congregation sits

pediment: triangular gables that appear over porches and often contain sculptures

piers: pillars supporting an arch or roof

seat: a center of authority

spherical: having a rounded shape

spires: long, tapered structures on the top of a church or building

stonemason: a person skilled in building with stone

surveyor: a person who examines and records the features of an area

transept: the part of a church that crosses the nave at right angles

turrets: small towers placed on top of larger towers

Index

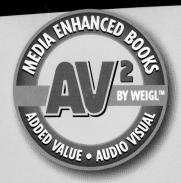

Log on to www.av2books.com

AV² by Weigl brings you media enhanced books that support active learning. Go to www.av2books.com, and enter the special code found on page 2 of this book. You will gain access to enriched and enhanced content that supplements and complements this book. Content includes video, audio, weblinks, quizzes, a slide show, and activities.

AV² Online Navigation

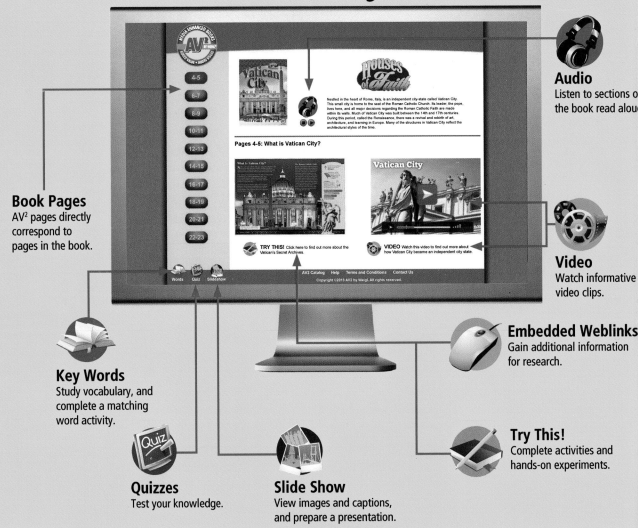

Audio
Listen to sections of the book read aloud

Book Pages
AV² pages directly correspond to pages in the book.

Video
Watch informative video clips.

Key Words
Study vocabulary, and complete a matching word activity.

Embedded Weblinks
Gain additional information for research.

Try This!
Complete activities and hands-on experiments.

Quizzes
Test your knowledge.

Slide Show
View images and captions, and prepare a presentation.

AV² was built to bridge the gap between print and digital. We encourage you to tell us what you like and what you want to see in the future.

Sign up to be an AV² Ambassador at www.av2books.com/ambassador.

Due to the dynamic nature of the Internet, some of the URLs and activities provided as part of AV² by Weigl may have changed or ceased to exist. AV² by Weigl accepts no responsibility for any such changes. All media enhanced books are regularly monitored to update addresses and sites in a timely manner. Contact AV² by Weigl at 1-866-649-3445 or av2books@weigl.com with any questions, comments, or feedback.